# ME & PHIL

## My Imaginary Friend

# ME & PHIL

## My Imaginary Friend

Poems by

Katie Darby Mullins

© 2023 Katie Darby Mullins. All rights reserved.
This material may not be reproduced in any form, published,
reprinted, recorded, performed, broadcast,
rewritten, or redistributed without
the explicit permission of Katie Darby Mullins.
All such actions are strictly prohibited by law.

Cover design by Shay Culligan
Cover image by Everin Casey

ISBN: 978-1-63980-315-6

Kelsay Books
502 South 1040 East, A-119
American Fork, Utah 84003
Kelsaybooks.com

Thanks to everyone who read and engaged with these poems; to my husband Andy, who has championed this project (and every project) from the beginning—you make it all worthwhile; to Grace, who reminds me that there is delight every day; to Charlie, who never fails to challenge and encourage me; to Corinna, who helped me shape this and take myself seriously; and to my mom, dad, sister, and heartsister, all of whom engage with my work with joy and fervor.

# Acknowledgements

*Atomic Flyswatter:* "Dr. Phil Asks About a High School Ex-Boyfriend," "The Poem Where Dr. Phil Is in Reruns"

*Atticus Review:* "Dr. Phil and I Take Down Halloween Decorations"

*Day One* (Amazon): "Dr. Phil and I Watch the Cubs Win, Over and Over"

*The Ending Hasn't Happened Yet:* "The Poem Where I Allow Dr. Phil to Interview Me," "Dr. Phil and Our Dislocated Shoulders"

*Glass: An Anthology of Poetry:* "Dr. Phil and I Watch My Husband Play Guitar in a Crowded Bar"

*Hobart* (now *HAD*): "The Poem Where Dr. Phil and I Have Lunch," "Dr. Phil and I Go to the Batting Cages"

*Okay Donkey:* "Dr. Phil Rides with Me to the Back Doctor"

*Rock & Sling:* "On the Set with Dr. Phil McGraw"

*Storyscape Journal:* "The Poem Where I Can See a Ghost, But Dr. Phil Can't"

# Contents

Dear Dr. Phil: Please Don't Get Cancelled
    Before I Sell This Book     13

## HAVE A GOOD SHOW, EVERYBODY

The Poem Where Dr. Phil and I Have Lunch     17
Dr. Phil and I Watch the Cubs Win,
    Over and Over     19
Dr. Phil Evaluates My Nickname,
    "Our Lady of the Sorrows"     21
On the Set with Dr. Phil McGraw     23
Dr. Phil and I Take Down Halloween Decorations     25
Dr. Phil Asks About a High School Ex-Boyfriend     26
Dr. Phil Grills Me About Another Ex-Boyfriend's
    Album (I Threw Away) Years Ago     28
The Poem Where Dr. Phil Is in Reruns     31
The Poem Where I Allow Dr. Phil to
    Interview Me     32

## TODAY IS GOING TO BE A CHANGING DAY IN YOUR LIFE

The Poem Where Dr. Phil and I Do the Dishes     37
Dr. Phil Looks Through My Internet History     39
Dr. Phil Asks About a Close Friend
    from High School     41
Dr. Phil Tries to Teach Me How to Listen     43
The Poem Where I Convince Dr. Phil to Sing
    "Oh! You Pretty Things" with Me at Karaoke     46
The Poem Where Dr. Phil Rides
    to the Back Doctor with Me     48
I Try to Explain to Dr. Phil That I Don't Want
    Babies, But Wish I'd Been Pregnant     49
Follow-Up Interview:
    After the Ehlers-Danlos Diagnosis     51

INTERMISSION WITH GUEST
   DAVID BOWIE

"You've Got to Wake Up"     55

THIS IS A SAFE PLACE TO TALK ABOUT
   HARD THINGS

| | |
|---|---|
| A List of Times I'm Pretty Sure Dr. Phil Possessed My Physical Therapist After My Stroke | 59 |
| Dr. Phil and Our Dislocated Shoulders | 62 |
| Dr. Phil and I Go to the Batting Cages | 64 |
| Dr. Phil and I Talk About Verbs | 66 |
| *Into the Woods* with Dr. Phil | 68 |
| Dr. Phil Questions My Big Life Decisions in Light of My Blinding Need for Perfectionism | 70 |
| The Poem Where I Can See the Ghost, But Dr. Phil Can't | 71 |
| I Become a Private Investigator (With Little to No Help from Dr. Phil) | 73 |
| Follow-Up Interview: On Sleeplessness, Possession | 77 |

I AM NOT GIVING UP ON YOU

| | |
|---|---|
| Dr. Phil and Me Before the War | 83 |
| Dr. Phil and I Pretend to Be Punks | 85 |
| I Try to Explain a Recurring Dream to Dr. Phil | 87 |
| Dr. Phil Rides Shotgun | 89 |
| Dr. Phil and I Go Back to 2001 (For a Minute) | 90 |
| Reading Over My Shoulder, Dr. Phil Asks Some Questions About Fire, Control | 93 |

Dr. Phil and I Watch My Husband Play Guitar
   in a Packed Bar   94
The Poem Where I Tell Dr. Phil He's Not Real   96

# Dear Dr. Phil: Please Don't Get Cancelled Before I Sell This Book

If you were to see me at the grocery store
My face would mean as much to you as
It does to me: nothing. Since my stroke,
I don't recognize the contours and freckles
I know were always there. You know me—

—you don't. I keep forgetting. We spent
So much time together on the page, you
Apparition, you pixelation, you charming ghost.
Perhaps I don't know myself. What I meant
Was that I cover my face in makeup and sunglasses
Everything bright or silly to make the stranger
In the glass feel like a friend. That's why you

Came around, anyway. I was having a hard time
Incorporating all my selves, and then there
You were, a haze of medications and Dallas
Accent piercing through in razor clarity,
Reminding me of home, warm and comforting.

I know it wasn't really you. I know

I created you from my own ribs, the ones
I removed so that I could try and see
If I could recognize my heart. After moving
Everything, it seemed so much easier to confess
Fear and anger and even hope to—well, you.
No audience, of course, though thanks for the interviews.

But Dr. Phil—real Dr. Phil, not the man who befriended
My fragmented brain—I need you to walk lightly.
Make good choices. We had some adventures,
And if you get cancelled, you may never know
If you helped put me back together again.
You may never know if you see me shopping
That you have walked those aisles with me,
Static and invisible, while I tried to remember
Exactly what it was I liked to eat.

HAVE A GOOD SHOW, EVERYBODY

# The Poem Where Dr. Phil and I Have Lunch

We both order steak. Medium rare. We glance
knowingly, exaggerating our Dallas accents
just slightly, our private joke about the meat.
I want him to know that we're the same:
that I'd rather be happy than right, that
sometimes, when I was scared at night, alone
in my drafty, uninsulated house, I turned
reruns of his show on as loud as I could,
letting that Texan swagger burst through tall ceilings
and hopefully out the windows. He helped
me pretend I was safe. That was a long time ago:
before I was married, before the fire. But now—

does anyone ever come to him without a problem?
I am asking him how to let go the slights I carry:
the stories people tell me about a woman who looks
like me: the pointed looks, my husband's ex: I can't stop
looking and finding hurt. *I could tell you stories,*
I say, but the details are all mixed up now,
now that someone is listening. Something about
how I'm *not a bad person, but*: something about
me being the *lowest common denominator*.
I blink, and then I own these shards of venom:
after the fire, I stopped holding on to physical
things, but pain, pain echoes and radiates, pain
electrocutes these bones. "I don't want to be like this,"
I start, but then he says, "First, lunch. We're friends."
(I've always thought we'd be friends.)

He's tall. No, taller than that. And he's well-dressed—
but I've come in my sweatpants. We don't have
an audience. And when he starts asking questions,
I'm magnanimous: *I know she must hurt,
I represent the things she's lost.*

He nods, and unlike his TV self,
he is quiet. I hand him pictures I found
when cleaning out the garage: he looks at her
terrified teenage stare, so mismatched
from the wedding dress, and I can tell that he is full,
deep sorrow pouring into him like a faucet.
"So much was destroyed," I said, "but these
pictures made it." The photo paper smells like ash,
but here it is. When he puts his arm around me,
it is like the blanket the neighbors brought
while I watched my house burn. When he sighs,
it is like the sound of the ceiling giving way.
And when he says, "Sometimes, you have to drop
the rope," I know it is true, because dammit,
I say it to myself over and over again.

But then he turns into my father. And then
my husband. Then a mirror. And it is me
telling me the things I've learned from seasons
of watching Dr. Phil. And there's smoke
in the background, and the steak has caught fire,
and I feel heavy and sad. But this is real life:
I change the channel, turn it up real loud.
Other people's problems ricochet off the walls,
and I always know how to help them. I guess
what Dr. Phil will say before the words cross
the threshold: *don't play semantics with me.*
And thank God for that sweet predictability,
the conversations I've pretended to have,
for the fake absolution the good TV doctor
always offers me, whether it's good TV or not.

# Dr. Phil and I Watch the Cubs Win,
## Over and Over

It's three days since the Cubs broke
the streak—my husband is working
overnight. Oncology floor. People
are dying around him constantly, now,
and somehow I have to coax myself
into sleep anyway, without his chest
rising and falling next to me. Usually,

I leave the TV on at night, muted voices
scaring away the shadows I worry
over in the dark. Dr. Phil is my go-to:
deep southern accent swaying in the space
above my head, protecting me with the fierce
sound of home. This week, though, ESPN

blares in the background, people crying
and hugging and singing "Go Cubs,
Go." Men at cemeteries with loved ones
who couldn't live long enough to see
the victory, but knew it was coming,
it had to come. I want this to last forever:

this joy, this friendship. But the coverage
is starting to be dotted with injury reports,
basketball games. And finally, when it starts
to fade out around 2 AM, Dr. Phil appears
at the foot of my bed. "This still?" he asks.

I can't explain that even though this isn't
my team, I need this: proof that no one
loses forever and curses
can end. But he doesn't press.

I crawl to the end of the bed and lie
down on my belly. We watch a few more
rounds of Eddie Vedder leading
a singalong. He nods at me and says,
"This is going to be somebody's year,"
and I think of the static in my bedroom,
the hospital where my husband walks
the halls at night, the people who learned
how easy it is for the body to fail.
How hard it can be to make it
all the way home.

# Dr. Phil Evaluates My Nickname,
## "Our Lady of the Sorrows"

We walk on uneven pavement, down stairs that lead nowhere,
passing dirt plots that, decades ago, were likely filled
proudly with flowers. "You lived here?" he asks, and everything
sounds like an interrogation. "Everyone lives somewhere,"
I say. "I was in grad school," I say. But the truth is, I liked
it: I liked the quiet (that I would only learn later could be pierced
with the occasional gunshot), I liked the restaurant down the street.
I liked the rust on the houses, how cheaply I furnished
a miserably hot duplex with Goodwill furniture and a table
my father bought at Target and painstakingly put together.

"Another guy lived down on 14th. We'd go to the gas station
and get donuts and sit on the nowhere stairs and go to the park."
Dr. Phil nods, like he approves of our morning routine.
I suddenly feel defensive: "I needed a break," I said. "Sometimes
I just need to walk." "Know the feeling," Phil says, hands deep
in his pockets. "Well, lead the way. There's an amphitheater?"

Here's where it gets funny. I remember the amphitheater, but not
if it's real. Let's say it is. It's better that way. Because
then I can say: "Sitting on this stage, this is where Nick told me
he thought of me as *Our Lady of the Sorrows,* because I could walk
into a room, make everyone feel better, and leave wrung out
like some kind of old sponge." So Phil and I sit, my feet dangling
so much higher up than his. I think of Bob Dylan as I realize I look
just like a little girl. And suddenly, Phil grabs my hand and says:
"You can only live that way so long."

"You know, once we found a stray cat?"
I'm deflecting. "It was clearly sick, skin and bones. My boyfriend
was allergic and I begged Nick to take him. Neither of us could,
not really. But I still think about the cat."

"You can't think about every lost soul and sleep at night,"
Phil says. I kick my Converse against the side of the stage,
silver glitter reflecting disco-ball sunlight. "I don't sleep much,"
I admit. He puts his arm around me and says, "You don't have
to be Our Lady of the Sorrows. That's not your only value."
Or maybe I want him—anyone—to be able to make me believe it.

# On the Set with Dr. Phil McGraw

I wake up in LA, fragrant
orange blossoms on the wind
and the studio gate is open,
waiting for me. Somehow I know
there's a front row seat

and Dr. Phil is expecting me. Today
he's interviewing a pageant mom,
someone who is obsessed
with performing her life. Her girls
are tiny clones of her, each

other. Dressed in taffeta-like cupcakes,
their faces will blur
on TV, but I can see that look
in their eyes, hungry, scared.
He talks to her about *need*

and what people do to fix
those broken parts. Why they cake
their children with makeup,
fake teeth. How that somehow
fills gaps left by lovelessness.

I can only approach this as who
I am: he says "need," I say "white whale."
I imagine this woman, perfect nails,
spearing a trophy off the side of a boat.
I hear the anxiety of desire.

Why does he need me here today?
Of course, the good doctor knows
what to say, how to say it: TV
compels a certain narrative. But
afterwards, he grabs Robin's

hand, then mine. We walk off stage
all three of us. And when he turns
to say, "Thank you for coming,"
I can feel his question in the way
he squeezes my hand: *how*

*am I different from her? Is my life
all played out for this audience?* I can't
comfort him. So much is built
for the camera. When the soft LA sun
hits my face in the parking lot,

I feel like I am everyone there: the girls
in heavy clothes, the mom who wants
so badly for them to matter—the doctor
who can't always answer his own questions.
The beloved wife, holding hands

down the soundstage hall, every day
moving out into the weather with certainty.
Of course—this walk, it's on camera, too,
it's all through a lens, fuzzed and faded
for network, clear as the sunset in person.

# Dr. Phil and I Take Down Halloween Decorations

Last year, I bought candy corn lights on sale;
so much easier to be festive once decorations
are in boxes for next year. But now, those lights
riddled with pollen and very real spiderwebs
twist their way around the posts on the porch.

The sweet stench of week-old jack-o-lantern
reminds me that decay is coming, and soon
the face will rot inward, caking the candle
with layers of useless, weather-worn fruit.
I hand Dr. Phil the lights as we weave
them in and out of the wooden slats and he winds
them around his forearm as we go. "Sometimes
I like the small tasks," I say. "It resets my brain,
focusing on something rote." He smiles.
"So many relationships could be saved like this,
handing small lights back and forth until the job
is done." I want to yell at him: can't we just *do*
this, not worry about what it means?

But I listen to the thick glass clink
as the bulbs hit each other, and decide
to just let him have this one: after all,
if I wasn't reaching for significance here,
would he keep coming back to me?

# Dr. Phil Asks About a High School Ex-Boyfriend

*When you base your whole identity*
*on a reaction against somebody*
*it's the same as being in . . .*
—Harvey Danger (Sean Nelson), "The Same As Being In Love"


I haven't thought about him in so long, I don't know
how to start: is the vague memory of ink stains
and the smell of cinnamon enough to build a character
I don't fully remember? But then, every once in a while,
I'll get a burst of a moment, loud like a headache, lit up
in clear day: today I remember his car, maybe a Nissan?
Oh, God. Silver in the sun, papers on the floorboard, always
green pen. Parked in front of his house, the flat roof—
then it's gone.

I can't figure out why, now, Dr. Phil wants to know—
"Who is this boy in the picture?"
                                "We all have albums full
of boys we don't talk to anymore," I say, waving him
away. The garage is crowded but the pictures are safe,
waterproof boxes. I try not to get lost out here, disappearing
into prom dress taffeta and vague forgotten faces. I don't
remember the girl in them, and I'm scared that she still
haunts this body. If I can't remember his face, maybe
she won't be able to show hers.

Phil smiles and says, "These people make us who we are,"
and I cringe, because he's nothing but an ending now: a journal
read and shoved back in my drawer, a CD left on a car seat,
just enough to remind me he could always pry open a door.
            "It's like a hot stove," I say. "Not so close."
But then I remember the feeling of trouble—knowing
that loving someone else was the worst risk I could ever take.
That even knowing someone loved me was dangerous.

And then that brilliant color of a memory,
when I told the boy in the pictures I hated the rain, and he reached
for me and pulled me out into it, and danced with me in the mist.
His leaning in close, telling me my eyes were Elysian Fields—
I smiled, all I could think of was how much I hated my clothes
growing ever damper against his chest, how much I couldn't wait
to let my thick hair down and loose for the car heater to dry.
How I made a quiet promise never to tell him how much
I had to pretend so that he would like me. A promise that if, God
forbid, he ever left, that I would not compromise like that,
    never again.

# Dr. Phil Grills Me About Another Ex-Boyfriend's Album (I Threw Away) Years Ago

*I lie about this,* I said, putting the CD
In the stereo (I can't *really listen* anymore:
It was in an old car, many disasters ago).
Dr. Phil rolls the windows down
And the smell of tall mown Indiana grass
And allergies mixes between us: shared air.

*You had to know,* he said. *One friend—
She said he smelled like a distillery.*
Of course, then he turned the music loud,
Tips of his mustache turning smile.

That summer was the youngest
I have ever been: even younger
Than when I was a kid. That summer
I believed a man who couldn't love
Would love me more than he
Loved to tell his own legend.

*I cried when he ended it,* I said.
Phil nods, begins to tell me it's normal,
And I say, *no, Phil, I begged.*

He starts the first track over, even though
I love the jubilance in the second song.
*You can't rewind to a specific moment,*
He says. *You have to remember
The whole thing.* It was kisses at parking lots
And handpicked flowers. It was him

Telling me, "I was married once," and me
Saying, "Don't say another word
Until this is over." It was late night
Radio shows and cherry tobacco wafting
From the neighbors.

*But you couldn't have that without*
*Being open, pretending to yourself—*
*Because make no mistake, girl,*
*You knew—that it was nothing real,*
*You only do something if you're getting something in return.*

I say along with him—"We only act a certain way
Because of a desired outcome,"
But what did I want then, the only
Summer I wore a bikini, the only
Time I ever really went from stranger
To partner? Phil goes to skip
Back to the beginning but I say,
*No. Let it roll this time. Let it wash over me.*

We drive through the decaying smell
Of dogwood trees, lit up and pink
And rotten, and I listen to a ghost:
Not the man, who I can't even picture anymore,
But my ghost, a woman blooming,
Trying to turn myself into someone lovable,
Someone strong when the man gets high, careens over
The console, crying to "Captain Jack"
My younger self thinking, "He just needs you,"

But I wasn't so stupid: even as I fell
Into the void, tried to learn what love was,
I knew that I was the most replaceable part
In a very familiar story he told, would tell
About every woman he knew. "I kept one
Promise," I told Phil, and he smiled: "I only
Have one story about a man like him."

# The Poem Where Dr. Phil Is in Reruns

Summer's lonely: the heat radiating off asphalt,
reflecting back at me when I look at my flip-flops.
I'm so much more used to staring at the TV
when I need to get out of my own mind, but even I
can't convince myself that I haven't seen today's argument
already—you know the one. The ex and his new woman,
stage left from his first wife, while they scream
about who screwed up their kids. (Kids who,
of course, are in the front row, faces tensed in pain.)
I must admit: I have probably seen this show twice,
but the fight, over and over, constantly, hundreds
of times, the same words, different faces, aging
in their bitterness. I try to conjure Phil, but he's gone—
vacationing somewhere I can't afford, even in dreams.

I'd like to ask him, though: why this story?
When your marriage has gone so well? Robin
sitting in the front row every day, polished and prim,
hair curled perfectly and never the same dress—
why do you bring so many broken people
to talk to each other this way in front of the world?
But I know why.

        We don't always come by our
obsessions honestly. Sometimes they are handed
to us, like some horrible torch. My dog pulls
at the leash, reminding me that the sidewalk
is hot, and she'd rather spend her time running
than standing still. I wish I could say I felt the same.

# The Poem Where I Allow Dr. Phil to Interview Me

I can say the first part: "Please take a seat.
Happy to meet you, sorry for the circumstance."
I'll nod, perfect eye makeup reflecting off the lens
of the biggest camera I've ever seen, mobile
and moving smoothly around us to catch every
angle. He'll smell like boots: the pleasant way
the pair smells when you first open the box
and you can still picture the factory in your mind.
He'll have already shown video of me to the audience:
they'll know I can't concentrate since the housefire,
not like before. That I have a webcam now
so I can show my stupid mind that the house
is still standing when I'm not there.

"What about at night?" he'll ask, and even though
I'm prepared for it, I'll still recoil, just a little.
Are you ever really ready to admit the things
you've spent years ignoring? "I still wake up
smelling smoke," I'll say. He'll reach out
a handkerchief, which of course, I don't need,
because no, I am not crying, and I will not be
crying, and I have never been crying, so I'll shove
it back towards him.
                    "Why are you so angry?"
he'll ask, and I know every answer is going to fall
like some horrible arrow, not pulled tight enough
in the bow. "Do you want people to feel sorry
for you?" Of course not, *of course not,*

but if I didn't, why would I tell anyone about
these nightmares? Why would I ever let anyone
close enough to know this happened, let alone
mattered? I'll choke out, "Everything's before
and after," and he'll nod, get out of his chair
and walk to me, hugging me with enormous arms.

I won't tell him that he smells like burnt leather.
I won't tell him none of this talking helped,
that even the illusion of relief is an insult.
I won't tell him that the moment is coming
back and that we all have to get out of the building,
get out, because now my eyes are stinging, watering,
and I am *not crying,* so it must be the smoke, it must be.

TODAY IS GOING TO BE A CHANGING DAY
IN YOUR LIFE

# The Poem Where Dr. Phil and I Do the Dishes

Dollar store dish soap fills the sink,
pink and artificial—grapefruit-scented.
I cannot believe the dishwasher broke
again. Suds sting bitten cuticles. Plates
slip and slide through my hands while TV
drones in the background, white noise,
my stepdaughter plugged into it
like it's a wall.

            There he is again: Dr. Phil
with a hand towel, offering to help me dry
the growing stack of wet silverware I've stacked
on the counter. He's pixelated, tinged slightly blue,
but the dogs don't bark: I don't question it.
I can always use the help. He takes a novelty
coffee mug with a squirrel on it and squeezes
his big hand inside the cup. "I've been thinking,"

I say out loud, "about how much love is too much:
can it really be healthy to turn yourself inside out?"
He smiles, but it's coy: "You know, 'parent' is a noun
and a verb." I watch my stepdaughter, but the sink
overfills, just a little. He swipes at the puddles
with his towel. "The words you use matter," he says,
"but you exist, too."

            I have read so many self-help
books about stepparenting. But sometimes, my gut aches
to override what I know, to be intimate, corded
together by something physical and real. Dr. Phil
must know what I'm thinking, and he puts a damp,
warm hand on my shoulder before he disappears.

For a moment, I worry I've recreated his advice
from years of watching him onstage, saying
the same platitudes to people more desperate than me.

The irony is not lost on me: the pixels fizzing out
like so much carbonation while sickening citrus
bubbles pop in the sink. Everything floats away
that's left untethered; even the things you watch
can evaporate before your eyes.

# Dr. Phil Looks Through My Internet History

I can't count how many times I've heard
him say, "People don't do things unless
they get something out of it." I try not
to question what I'm getting now,
        scrolling through a list
          of usual suspects, people whose lives
          are so tangential to mine
as to not even exist in the same story. And yet: refresh.
Some high school detective. Soda pop freak.
Keeping tabs and finding court records.
Not my business, but not hidden well enough
to be a secret. The trouble. I'm hooked.

I try to ignore Phil's ghostly hand on my tense
shoulder, his quiet disapproval of my work.
I tell him, "I don't know why I do this," but
        the only thing that makes me
        strong now, now with so much gone
in a haze of smoke, is the power to know what
people want—*need*—left alone and private.
I have to know the whole narrative because
I can't see my own damned arc through the ash.

He just purses his lips, shakes his head.
But he reads over my shoulder and we
cluck together to see an enemy's long-ago ex
was the recent victim of violence, some gun
thing, no injury, but a hell of a lot of brandishing
        and noise. He shudders when
          I go through death and divorce,
            only vaguely aware of the periphery
of my social group. But then, I click to Facebook,
and he shuts the computer, tells me to go to bed. No good—

*no good* comes of looking at the shadows in the cave, not when you are still chained here, still chained in darkness, still surrounded by the phantom smell of flames.
But just because the computer is closed and I'm in bed doesn't make the flames leave. They just tickle underneath, waiting for me to be drawn back.

# Dr. Phil Asks About a Close Friend
## from High School

"Thailand is so far away, he is actually
Living in tomorrow," I tell Dr. Phil, feeling poetic.
I was folding laundry—my PT wants it to be therapeutic,
First cross left. Then right. No more stress.
Dr. Phil smiles, takes a handful of socks to ball
Together, makes them easier to find on dark
Mornings. "I'm not sure that's how it works,"
He says, but he smiles. "So why call him? Why now?"

I allowed Mahmood to really leave after high school;
Some people are destined for excitement,
And I knew he'd already learned so much about loss.
"I didn't want to be Dallas for him," I said.
"I don't care why *now*."

My shoulder hurts. I know it shouldn't,
But I don't know that it will ever fit right again,
Not since I dislocated—relocated—it on a plane.
I rub the gap between my shoulder blade and back—
An "angel's wing," someone once called it,
A deformity caused by scoliosis. I notice Dr. Phil
Take a slightly larger pile of laundry.

"We had a lot of different memories," I said.
"He didn't make me talk about anything."
Phil nodded. "But you did?"
The demons always creep in. Phil knows. But—
Mahmood always had this way
Of talking over, or under, or through it
Like it was just normal.

"He reminded me that I made or gave him some kind of ring," I
said. "That when his mother died, I told him
things would never be the same.
I needed to hear those words back."

"For you? Or for him?"
But I don't know. I turn the TV on. Some movie.
Phil grabs the remote. "You were 16," he said.
"You did your best."
I have to sit down, just for a minute. I will,
I will finish this load, dammit.

"I don't remember giving him a ring," I say, "but
He brought me one back from Bangladesh—
I still have it. It survived the fire." Phil sits next to me,
Mutes the screaming TV,
Puts his ghost-weight hand
On my shoulder, which lights up.
It's like a butterfly landing,
Which of course, can change everything.

"It reminded me of when everything was intense, raw—"
But Phil's gentle touch crawled through me somehow
And I knew, just for a moment,
That softness and strength could live together,
That the birth of autonomy and a life—
One with no restrictions, not yet—
Was not our life anymore. Those days—skipping
Lunch to sit on his truck in the rain,
No decisions fully made yet, no mistake that couldn't be fixed—
That was gone. "We were never going to be people
Who could just skip lunch and have an easy life, were we?"
"A part of you always knew that," Phil says, slowly sneaking still
Unfolded laundry back to the basket for tomorrow.

# Dr. Phil Tries to Teach Me How to Listen

*Those 5A bastards run a shallow cross*
*It's a boy's last dream and a man's first loss*
      —Jason Isbell, "Speed Trap Town"


We were the 5A bastards with a Dallas zip code,
And I didn't understand how different that was
From big-time high school Ohio games
Which could be 2A and still give men their names.

So we watched my husband's old high school secure
A bid on TV—the boys from the "Burg" heading to state,
And I told him, "I wish I could feel that
Moment, its potency: teenage
Passion, the strength of a last
Play out of enemy territory
Into the end zone." He looked

Far away, and he said he knew
How they felt, that it was the highlight
Of a life spent recounting that last
Football smashed into the ground
Under shadows of high school parents
And the goal posts, not so
Different from the crosses lit up
And shadowing in so many yards.

I told him in Texas, that's not it,
And he said, "This isn't Texas,"
Years I've spent thinking I knew how
Football worked in Ohio's speed trap towns
The small hamlets and villes
That my husband grew up in.

How can I have missed something
So simple for so long? That my district packed
With 5A teams and boys who become men while still
Donning pads and crashing into
Each other like bright marbles
Is so different from his small school
Where even though he hasn't gone there in decades
He knows the last names of kids on the roster?

I need to stop talking
To fill in gaps, I need to stop calling audibles,
Stop juking mid-sentence, to wait
To hold up my silence like an offensive line
So my husband has enough time in the pocket
To get the play off. He thinks so deeply.

Dr. Phil is here, though, and he nods,
Maybe leading by example,
Maybe blocking for me so that I will
Shut up long enough to learn
What 2A public schools mean in America now
And the frustration that comes
With that first success of manhood,
What happens if it's the last one.

My husband got out. Sometimes I worry
He doesn't feel that way, that I remind
Him of ways he is stuck: in a holding pattern
With someone who talks
When he takes a breath.

Andy finally falls asleep, and Dr. Phil
Leans over my bedside at my in-laws' house,
So tall he has to bend at the waist,
And he says, over the distant rumble of trains,
The smoldering fires burning out
On their own in the horizon:
"You know it's a problem. Now
You have to fix it. I can't
Do it for you." We both watch
As my husband's chest rises and falls
Built by the Midwestern grit
That seemed so attractive to me on TV,
And in him. Dr. Phil says,
"You can't know what you don't know."
He fades into the darkness
And I'm left in a bedroom that is familiar,

Like my own, but not, and I promise
Myself that tomorrow I will not
Fill every space with noise,
That I will learn to listen for sounds
In the distance.

# The Poem Where I Convince Dr. Phil to Sing "Oh! You Pretty Things" with Me at Karaoke

First, you think you know how we sound
But you don't—you don't know my voice
At all, how serious I take it, how I strut
With no humor, pretending for a moment
I've ever been a rebel, ever been the Leper Messiah.

Second—you think you hear him questioning
Lyrics, reading off the screen. Wrong.
He knows it, and instead of laughing out,
"Don't you know you're driving your mommas
And papas insane?"
He sings with the gentle conviction of someone
Who knows the danger of being pretty
Because he's seen it all before, mascara run
Down sharp cheeks on those tall chairs.

I used to sing "Night Moves" when I was alone—
Everyone always claps you back
Into that last chorus, on the 2 and the 4,
The 1 and the 3, everyone's having fun.
Tonight, I can tell only half of the patrons
Have passing knowledge of the song,
Only half have passing knowledge it is karaoke night.

"This is why you exist," I tell Phil, breathless, when we sit down.
Am I on blood thinners yet? No. That's later.
So maybe I have a whiskey.
He looks confused (and drinks water),
But I say, "I couldn't write about you
Until I realized the art I loved best
Was from people who, instead of doubting instinct,
Became the alien." He shakes his head,

And I think he's going to ruffle my hair,
But I realize: I don't sing karaoke anymore.
I haven't in a decade, since I lived
In Ohio, and went to that little railroad car bar.
Dr. Phil looks real, but I am a projection,
Something phoned in. And that swagger,
The stage confidence—that was a ghost, too.
How did I get here? How did this nightmare—
But then, I can still hear it. And you still can't.

# The Poem Where Dr. Phil Rides
## to the Back Doctor with Me

Sometimes I imagine my vertebrae like explosions,
Each piece a tiny mushroom cloud lit up
In gray and blue and maybe even purple—
Loud colors and pain streaking, catching fire.

Today my shoulder is erosion: a shelf worn
Down from overuse. Something's
Wrong, but I'm supposed to pretend I don't
Notice. Power of positive thinking. Doctors
Have told me since I was ten that I didn't hurt,

"And thank God all this pain doesn't hurt,"
I say out loud. Dr. Phil is in the passenger seat,
Trying to keep his expensive shoes off the papers
On the floorboard. He's come to accept

The mess. Some matchbox twenty song is on the radio,
And I can tell he's torn between fidgeting
With the dial (—and me shutting him down) and singing.
"I see your pain. And I can't begin to understand

How you feel," he says. It's a canned answer,
But a good one: sometimes I wonder if the swelling
Goes down a little every time someone
Believes me. I've seen him say this to widows,
People who've lost parents. And in the scheme

Of things, I know this isn't so bad: but sometimes
All that knowledge courses through my muscles
And they tense up harder, and soon, my body
Is knotted with pieces of me I can't even name.
Sometimes I'm carrying the pain of the whole
World in the worn-out spaces between bones.

# I Try to Explain to Dr. Phil That I Don't Want Babies, But Wish I'd Been Pregnant

When my husband and I decided
Not to have any more children,
Just my stepdaughter, we were at a rest stop
Somewhere in Kentucky or Ohio
Somewhere between home and surgery
And we high-fived. By then, I'd had the premonition
Living in me for years: that I couldn't,
That the unexplained bleeding
In an Illinois hospital during a blizzard
*Had to have been—*
                        I've never said it,
And I won't. But that day, I was relieved
Because I was afraid I couldn't give
Him what his first wife could, what he
Wanted: a child. We talked occasionally
About Jacob and Rachel, but of course
There is another mother in that story, too.

"I do not want a baby," I say to Dr. Phil.
We have bounced back into a picture
Of Grace at Chuck E. Cheese, and the machines
Seem to be alive again, buzzing with noise,
And Dr. Phil seems delighted in watching her run
From machine to machine with manic
Glee, the first foray into learning
The thrill of the big payoff, the gamble.
"No," he says. "You can't." We know
Now: my hips could split and never return,
And that's not the worst-case scenario.
I watch a young Mexican woman talk
In soft Spanish to a baby she is wearing
On her chest. "I don't even want that,"

I say, and I know he thinks I'm lying.
He picks up the pizza crusts of Grace's plate
And eats them, probably to avoid saying
Something stupid about pregnancy to a woman.
About my biological clock—an alarm I turned off
Years ago—about how it will always be different
Because I don't know what it's like to have "my own,"
Like people haven't been telling that lie for years.

Grace runs back to the table, smelling faintly
Like someone I've never met, like she could
Never have been mine. She takes a swig of fruit punch
And kisses me, says, "I love you, KK,"
And then takes off back into the arcade, leaving
Fistfuls of worthless gray tickets
On the table. I tear up from the memory,
And I say, "It's none of the baby stuff—
But I don't know what it's like to feel
Life inside me." It sounds dumb when I say
It like that, but Phil takes both of my hands
In just one of his; he seems bigger today.
We are in a moving picture, anything can
Happen, and for a second,
I feel something kick me deep in the ribs.

# Follow-Up Interview:
## After the Ehlers-Danlos Diagnosis

He does not bring out my embarrassing secrets—
He's not asking why I played with toy horses until
I was almost out of high school,
Building elaborate apartments for them
Out of bookshelves in my walk-in closet,
Or why those imaginary friends I pretended
Were funny were actually a comfort,
Someone to talk to when I knew people thought
I was crazy. He's not concerned by my rituals—
"As long as they don't interfere with your life,"
He says, watching me brush my hair the hundredth
Time today, watching me flip through a book
I am not reading just to smell the pages.
And he doesn't care that still, when the wind
Takes my long hair and wraps it around
My face, I want to throw up because
I cannot stand it I can *not I cannot.*

He gently asks questions about the matter
At hand, which, right now, is the failing
Genetics, the way the collagen meant to hold joints
Tight, in my body, is not woven right,
Allowing them to fall out of socket, out of place.
"How many times did you sprain your ankle?
How many doctors?"
The answer is the same: seventeen.
*At least the right ankle.* But Dr. Phil can't help
My body, a wooden puppet held by strings.
"How does this make you feel?"

I have dreaded this. I'm still lying. I haven't
Broken or sprained that ankle seventeen times,
And I don't plan on telling him a real number.

"Katie?" He prompts. I have so many smartass answers—
"Special—it's rare," or "sore," or "tired,"
And those eke closer to the truth,
But the truth is when I first got diagnosed
I felt high with the pleasure of knowing
I'd been right for decades. Something was wrong.
And then by the next morning, I was furious with loss.
Lost time, lost possibilities.
I tell him, "I don't know how I feel."
He shrugs. We've talked through so many things,
And he seems to think
I'm stonewalling him. But I'm not—
I just don't know how to say, "Now I feel everything all the time,"
I don't know how to say, "I'd already decided
Not to have a baby, but now I don't have a choice."
Because some of the things that bother me
Don't make sense.

So we clamber down from those big chairs
(How was I able to get up there anyway,
Legs still unstable as Bambi without Valium?),
And he extends a hand. We walk
The same path he walks with his wife
After every show, but he doesn't hold
My hand. He gently places his on my back,
Guiding me toward the door, and instead
Of him laughing like he and his wife always do,
I look up at his face and see blankness.
No one seems to know what to say
In the face of pain, especially forever pain.
I wonder which one of us is more
Relieved to leave the soundstage.

# INTERMISSION WITH GUEST DAVID BOWIE

# "You've Got to Wake Up"

> *Take your protein pills and put your helmet on*
> *Commencing countdown, engines on.*
> *Check ignition—and may God's love be with you. . . .*
>      —David Bowie, "Space Oddity"

It's true. The stars look very different today:
Here am I, trapped in Neuro ICU,
And every single object in my visual path
Is in at least duplicate. Some things wind
Around themselves like invasive species
Or fly lenses. I can't tell.
      The nurses don't
Complain, though I think around the 3 AM
Vitals, they're becoming more and more
Disturbed by my Bowie playlist, "I'm Afraid
Of Americans" echoing down the hallway.

I feel like there's an arrow between my eye
And the back of my brain. That's a stroke.
You fix it with so much medicine, I have no
Real comprehension of what happened there.

"You've got to wake up—"

*But this is Major Tom to Ground Control . . .*
My parents fly in from Dallas. My husband
Stays up all night, monitors my breathing.
Friends take shifts. I don't remember who
To write the thank-you notes to, but I do
Remember the nurse, Theresa, who brought
Me a psychedelic elephant stuffed animal,
Tells me to call it Ziggy.
    *"You've got to wake up."*

Constant vitals. Are the blood thinners too much?
Is she fading? I start thinking of myself in the third
Person, *floating in the most peculiar way.* She is the girl
Who tells the night nurse, stop, listen, *really listen*
To the Mick Ronson solo with the Spiders from Mars,
Just through "Moonage Daydream."

The voice gets louder. "Katie, you have to wake up."
I went to the ER with a headache. I'm awake, I think.
But there he is, Dr. Phil, somehow on TV even though
I know it is not his programming time. "Katie—wake up."
I don't know yet all the things I'll learn:
That the veins in my eyes look like trees when light
Shines at them in a dark room, that it lines up with the story
Of Jesus curing the blind. I don't always tell people that
In the other eye—the "bad" eye—there were ghosts in the trees.
"What if this is it?" I ask Dr. Phil, or David Bowie, or God.
                      "Wake up," he says.

THIS IS A SAFE PLACE TO TALK ABOUT HARD THINGS

# A List of Times I'm Pretty Sure Dr. Phil Possessed My Physical Therapist After My Stroke

1. every time I say my "bad" side
Ryan says "don't think about it
like that. right and left."
but it is bad. or worse. it can't
hold pens securely and sometimes
I can't feel it at all, and I pretend
it is just the ground-up dust from colorful
blue and yellow butterfly wings, lovely
and impractical but bright.

but sometimes I can still mostly
use chopsticks and sometimes
I can still throw a seven-pound medicine ball
while balancing on a horrible tilting surface

Ryan says, "that side is stronger
than you think. don't sell yourself short."


2. when I fall at the end of a hard rep of exercises
Ryan will not let me do it just one more time
"you have to learn to fail," he says
and I didn't fall hard. that's not
what this is about. I need
to end on a high note. he says

"guess what? that's not always how it goes. you still succeeded."
I call Ryan names in the car.
but I feel better the next time I fall.

3. when he asks if I am in pain, I close my eyes
and search for the usual spots: shoulder,
back, neck, hips, knees, ankles. fine.
when I open my eyes, he's smiling. "you're reconnecting
your body with your brain. you've hurt
for so long that you have to be intentional
to figure out where the pain is."
I want to tell him the pain is in my ass
because even though I like him
I can't fully believe that this will work.

"it's good to know where it hurts," he says.
"someone with hypermobility usually can't
locate the source of their pain."
I pretend that Ryan is Dr. Phil. maybe he is for a minute.
"I have a hard time acknowledging anything
That isn't acute," I say.


4. he wants to know about my synesthesia—
he talks about empathy and '90s rock
and he lets me distract myself
from harder exercises by telling him
stupid stories about the grunge scene
and he always smiles and says *I never knew*
and *you know so much about.*
I look forward to seeing him. I spend time
trying to make sure I have a good
conversation topic if things start to hurt.

when I don't? he asks about the colors around us,
and I paint his room, lined with bright windows
with outrageous primary and secondary colors
I've come to associate with the place
and he hands me weights a little heavier
this time, and sometimes
I get it and sometimes I fail
and we swirl around, tilting on
uneven surfaces, trying to reteach
a body that feels little but vertigo
how to move with the colors
that are spinning so wildly above my head.

# Dr. Phil and Our Dislocated Shoulders

*In late February during some time off, Dr. Phil, practicing a dirt bike trick with some of his Hollywood stuntman friends, landed awkwardly and dislocated his shoulder and dinged up a few ribs . . .*
    —Fox News, in an article called "Dr. Phil kept serious dirt bike accident secret for months," published May 10, 2018

I wish mine had been a dirt bike accident:
The skid of concrete and skin, realization
You've pushed too far, you are only human,
You Icarus, you Achilles, you fly too close,
You lean into your weakness.
                    I dislocated my shoulder
After the best week of my life as I boarded
The plane back to Nashville, to drive home—
I reached back for the seat belt and heard
A sickening pop. But you heard the pop, too,
Didn't you? Or did it get caught in the noise
Of the accident, crunching metal, other bones
Jamming and breaking away from their muscles
Like flies given a second chance out of the web.

Was it your first time? It wasn't mine. I leaned
Into my husband with the bone out, so he could
Feel the cup of my empty joint, and said, "It's out
Again." I knew the strength it was going to take
To shove it back in was more emotional than physical.
I couldn't ask him to do it, I just needed a witness.

Dr. Phil, I need you. I have so many questions.
Now, now you go silent. You don't want to answer.

I've dislocated ribs, too. Does that help? Will you
Tell me about how long you were laid up?
Can you tell me how to feel now that I know
I will never, never stop dislocating things?

I can minimize the impact, but I have a parking
Pass that won't expire. I'm 31, Dr. Phil. I had a stroke.
You know that. You've sat in my hospital
Bed while I was too blind to watch your show.
I get the impulse to hide it. I hid for so many years.

I can't hide anymore. And you're still there, steady
As dying crickets in the middle of fall, swept
In the corner of Albertson's, the most visceral
Memory of my childhood in Texas. You light
My cortexes up like hearing and smell but today

I'm getting nothing, Dr. Phil. And we're
Almost the same—is it too close?
Did they make you do rehab on it, too?
Did you pretend it was a Tommy John
Injury like I did? Could you breathe
Without that rib digging into your lung—
Or is that because of my crooked back?
I need answers, Dr. Phil. I need to know
How close this was, if you get it now.

# Dr. Phil and I Go to the Batting Cages

> *The bullet is already in the brain . . . But for now Anders can still make time. Time for the shadows to lengthen on the grass, time for the tethered dog to bark at the flying ball, time for the boy in right field to smack his sweat-blackened mitt and softly chant,* They is, they is, they is.
> —Tobias Wolff, "Bullet to the Brain"

"The feeling of aluminum ringing up through your wrist
When you hit the sweet spot
Because you can always clip it and get to first—
But that vibration, that's the game,"
I say, but Dr. Phil isn't listening. He chooses a wooden
bat, something I never tried, and he is far away.
I try to remember the line from that old Tobias
Wolff story: what was it that kid said so wrong,
so pure, on the baseball diamond that it had been worth
a last thought?

                But I couldn't remember much. We
weren't really there. I just needed to get out
of the hospital, and I brought us here. I want to remember
how it feels to have a ringing in your wrist, victory
in your legs as you take a final lap. I hadn't moved
for days. I kept having dreams where people would
laugh and tell me I hadn't had a stroke, but I'd still
wake up, no feeling in my right side, confused.

Dr. Phil never lied to me. He never tried to convince me
that everything was normal. But when things were normal,
twenty years ago, before I knew there was something wrong,
baseball seemed safe enough. Something about that moment
where you know everything is OK, the soaring leather,
the smell of the spring grass kicked up by neon cleats.

"Say something," I beg. He picks up his Louisville
Slugger, runs his thick fingers up and down the polish,
and finally motions for me to come over to him. I want
him to envelop me, hug my whole body. Want to become
part of him, for part of him to possess my right side,
to move my hands and legs with the certainty of an authority
figure. He doesn't touch me. He says, "This will take a while—
but you know how the aluminum feels. You know the ringing.
Take this." He hands me his bat, and I wonder if he means
for me to hit a ball or something else. But he trudges out
to the pitching mound, all in a three-piece suit, and slow-pitches
the baseball my way.

      Nothing is real in hospitals, and the closest
to memory you have is the dreams, mostly morphine
and Ambien. But the truth is this: I felt that wood, and it didn't
ripple in my hands. There was no strange vibration. I hit
dead center, right over Dr. Phil's head, and he smiled while
my hands felt nothing, nothing at all. And I wondered: is this it?
Is my last moment of purity going to be a solid hit
but with no feeling?

      "You're going to be fine," he said, "But
I want you to know: a home run doesn't have to sting."
Too tired to run, I just dropped the bat, and it thunked
against the sand, smell of fresh cut grass wafting up.
Too tired to tell him I missed the sting, the best part.

# Dr. Phil and I Talk About Verbs

"Feelings are nothing until
You put verbs in your sentences,"
Dr. Phil always says—but
The problem is what verbs?
Always. Too grandiose and you
Alienate. Too extreme and you
Lose progress. "Hurt" doesn't
Count as a helping verb—
I am hurt. I am hurting. But—
I hurt, well, that counts. He nods.

But what about "respect"? I tell
Him he is a bouncer for hurt people
And he needs that word more
And I talk about words like "hatched"
And "slithered" and "broke" because
These are the words I keep finding—
Those and "burned." I tell him now
I listen for the noun too: I had—
God—had?—*so weak*—a stroke.

"What about choose?" he asks
"What about Have and Hold?" I ask.
So many subjects follow: in fire, in sickness,
In court. He says *you chose this path
And it is beautiful.* I tell him
We can't use nothing words like
*Beautiful,* which means different things
To different people. He thinks a moment
And says, "You chose this path.
It matters." That's the echo I let ring,

Roll around in my head at night,
Holding stuffed animals from nurses,
Waiting to see if my face ever looks
Like mine to me again. I let it reverberate
Deep in my ears, the places that already
Lost hearing from sitting on amps at concerts.
Silent, first. Then: *it matters, it matters.*
I try not to criticize the indirect pronoun—
I need *it* to apply to everything.

## *Into the Woods* with Dr. Phil

> *Grace suffered from the often underestimated and misunderstood disease of depression. From the time she was diagnosed at age 11, until her death, she struggled. She would tell her family that she could never feel anything. She couldn't feel all the love from everyone around her. Most tragically, she couldn't even feel the love for herself. She couldn't feel the fierce, undying love of her best friend, her mother Sue. When the disease finally overtook her, she will never know how many people loved her and will miss her . . .*
> —Dallas actor Grace Loncar's obituary

When the curtains part, the stage lights blind
even the most accustomed actor. I remember
it as looking into a dark, unforgiving ocean,
undulating in front of you, prepared to judge.
Then you smile. You start the scene or the song.
The narrator says, *Once upon a time,*
      And the beautiful, flaxen-haired Cinderella
sings back, as if she doesn't notice him at all:

*I wish . . .*

They go back and forth; they go *Into the Woods.*
Cinderella's wish made clear: she wants to go
to a festival, to fall in love. Even as a teen, I knew
that story rarely stayed a fairy tale.

Did Grace ever sing those lines? She acted
on so many of the stages I did when I was in Dallas,
performing watered down children's versions
of Sondheim. But this is the Internet era now,
baby: everyone's singing "Hey, Big Spender"
and putting on their best Russian Red lipstick
for an Instagram pout. *And she was sixteen,*
I keep telling Dr. Phil. And he keeps reminding me—
*And you didn't know her.*

*But I wish . . .*

Maybe she was never Cinderella, though the eyes,
magnified in her obituary, wide-open and clear,
her hair, simple blonde ringlets to her waist—maybe
she was Little Red Riding Hood, trying so hard
to find something that made her *feel* something,
even if that thing was scared—well, *excited* and scared.
Dr. Phil reminds me again *you don't know her,* but I knew
a version of her: a much less savvy, less curated
version. I knew what it felt like to don greasepaint
and wait for the audience to see you—because
*dammit, you can't be invisible under a spotlight,*
and because even if you aren't singing the big parts,
you're going to get a line out of it. Some kind of bump.

    "You don't act anymore," Phil reminds me,
like I'd even consider sliding back on to that plywood
and buffered floor. "This is obsessive behavior.
You've got to stop thinking of her." But for days,
I wonder: Is it because it could have been one of my friends?
Because she's from home? Because her father OD'd
in an expensive sports car a few days later?

Sometimes, when it gets really quiet, and I can't
get her off my mind—when I scroll through her
Twitter feed or Facebook (as her obituary encourages),
I see the sharp-tongued, wizened teen I would have
idolized. So edgy. And Phil, in his infinite wisdom,
tells me I need a mantra to get myself out of the feedback loop.

So I picture Grace, alone on a stage, light just reflecting
off her ringlets and red pout, matching her cape,
sitting alone with her long legs dangling from the edge,
singing those iconic last lines in Little Red's song:
"Isn't it nice to know a lot! . . . and a little bit not."

# Dr. Phil Questions My Big Life Decisions in Light of My Blinding Need for Perfectionism

"Why do you choose a life of rejection—a writer,
A second wife, a stepmom, a life where everything
You are seems to have an adjective in front of it
That means you always come in second place?"

I don't remember if he asked it, or if I did.
Maybe my PT asked. My husband? My friend?

I'm sure I said, "You don't understand."
I'm sure because I don't understand, either,
Except that it never feels like losing.

Most days, I watch my husband's eyes follow
Me around rooms with more beautiful women,
His gaze never fluttering. I watch my stepdaughter
Search for me in crowds. And sometimes,
When it's quiet enough, I spend time with Dr. Phil,
Who is sort of here, who couldn't have chosen me.
I know better than to think I'm the first choice.

So that's what gets me out of bed now—
The reaching. Even as my body fights
And succumbs to side effects, stumbling, drug-
Addled, I have to do some*thing* to matter.

"You aren't what you do," the voice I've come
To know as Dr. Phil whispers. It can't be
My own voice: I can say these words,
But I don't believe them. Not yet.

# The Poem Where I Can See the Ghost, But Dr. Phil Can't

One woman dressed in Victorian clothing,
weeping on the side of my bed. Children
in my backyard, flinging sticks, muffled
shouts. Accented voices down the hall
with champagne corks popping, creating
pockets of sound. No one else was there,
you know. But the contagion of my belief
has always been powerful. Those aren't

      the only ghosts. I see shadow
forms constantly. And tonight, I am laying
completely still in bed, watching a rugged
half-man walk through my room, slowly,
examine the fabrics of my hanging clothes,
move through the pill bottles by the bed.
My hair skates past my ear when he gets
close; I'm sure it's his long, cold fingers,
and I swear I can hear him whisper, "Shh,"
and my body is rotten with terror. I can't
breathe. An episode of *Dr. Phil* blares,

white noise to keep the visions at bay,
and he is shouting at a woman that she
*has* to look, she *has* to face her problem,
watch her decaying anorexic sister
talk about drugs on the big TV in front
of her. Or he can't help. Not if she ignores
the problem. I try to focus on his hands.

  I shouldn't be surprised when he
turns to face me, when he tries to talk
me out of my delusion: "This isn't real,
Katie," he is saying, but I know listening
to a TV doctor isn't any saner than giving
into the muscular anxiety of an ethereal
intruder. I am rigid with cold and I try
to let myself be talked out of living
a waking nightmare, of knowing, against
all odds, that this is it for me. "I don't see
anything," he says, and I repeat those words
*I don't see anything* inside myself while I watch
the man possess my space. I have always allowed
the unreal to inhabit me, to live in me, to create
shadows on my wall, to reach out from the TV.
I have welcomed this tangled up noise
and drawn it into myself, ghosts like a cloak,
because belief feels better than nothing.

# I Become a Private Investigator
## (With Little to No Help from Dr. Phil)

So I don't know who I'm hired to find,
But I can't care: I *need* this.
It's all finally happening like I planned—
The glitter of LA fades to haunted orange
Streetlamp glow; the beach holds
Nothing but nothing, closed and empty
And endless. I'm in the driver's seat,
Hanging my long-lens camera out
The window, resting it on the mirror,
Waiting to catch the cheaters or runaways I've been paid
To find. The dingy motel is exactly
What it was in my dreams, rain-
Soaked and filthy. The motel letters
Are jumbled; half the bulbs
Burned out. Burn out. *Come on,* I say.

Dr. Phil is lying down in the backseat.
I was mad at him for a while: how could he
Not support me? Maybe he was tired?
When he finally does talk, I shush him—
Like there's anyone around, like they could hear.

"Not all knowledge is good," he says. "Remember
How it felt the first time you realized
You could break into your father's email?"
I focus on even breath. He wants me to feel guilt.
"I was exhilarated," I admit. "Gleeful."
          "But what you found?" he says. I pretend
I don't remember that part of the story.
"Why are we really here? You've figured out
How to get into the court's system—just look up—"

"I have a code," I say. "No one I love. Nothing that hurts me."
Every time I type the name of a friend
Into the box that reveals backgrounds,
I lose a little faith. I can't do it anymore.

"Codes don't mean anything when you're hungry,"
Phil says. "You're starved for information. Do you
Know what you are looking for?"
The moon hangs like an ornament decorating
The sea foam green and pastel pink
Of the hotel sign, and finally, a door opens.
I rush to press the buttons, almost forgetting
How to use something analog.
I take as many pictures as I can, even though
Only one person is leaving.
She looks confused, but drives away.

"It's got to be her I'm hunting," I say,
Plugging my camera into my laptop. I feel
The warmth of the machine on my lap,
Moments away from a payoff. I know
This will never be about the money for me—
It is only about knowing secrets
That no one wants *me* to know. Phil sits up
And leans through the center console.

"Are you sure you want to know?"
But as he asks, the images appear, and I see
A small, braced and bandaged version of myself—
Not younger, but someone who still
Thinks suffering is an occasional event
And not something that can move in, become comfortable.

In every picture, I am holding a body part—
My wrist, my neck, my hip. I look miserable.

"You haven't connected back with her yet," Phil says.
"She's not gone, not forever—but you're not ready
To face yourself, to learn how to tell
Yourself what is about to happen, how much
Your life will change."
                   "So in this world," I say, "the stroke
Hasn't happened yet? I still think I'm crazy?"
He nods and looks at me. "You can't face her.
That's the danger of too much knowledge—
You can't always act on it."

I don't tell him that the strangest moment
In recovery was a dream where I was in New York,
Sandwiched between my husband and my friend
Adam, who was wearing an old coat and a hat
An ex-girlfriend made him, and Adam kept laughing,
Kept saying, "Can you believe they really thought
You had a stroke?" When I woke up, I could still
Barely move. I didn't cry but I wanted to. Phil shakes
Me back: "Are you OK?" he asks.

"Why would I go to this seedy hotel
By myself?" Phil smiles. "You might not be able to talk to her,
But you always know how to find people.
You knew this was how you would want to be found."
And it was so true it burned.

I wanted to be on both sides of that lens,
Someone who had a secret and someone who could
Expose it. I always wanted to be captured

In the strange nighttime hue of LA,
In a hotel no one had been in for years. I knew
I needed to play roulette with my safety—

Probably because even that younger Katie
Knew everything was going to change, and soon.
Phil lies back down and says,
"You'll always know where to find yourself."
I was going to ask him if I should follow me,
But he says, "It's been a long night, Kiddo."
And as I put the car in drive (my first car, a teal
Chevy Beretta I totaled a month into ownership—
How can it be this car?), I can feel
The distance between who I was

And who I am shift, come closer and further
Like the waves on the ocean. One minute
It was like we were still the same,
The next, I am looking at a ghost.
"Will I ever be just one person again?" I ask Dr. Phil.
"You already are," he says. "You just have to integrate
Her a little slower. And maybe if you
Stop hanging around motels and parks
Waiting to catch a glimpse,
She'll come to you when she's ready."
I instinctively touch my camera, my laptop—
My weapons. Because I can always find what I want
If I look hard enough, I can find where to look. But maybe—
    —maybe Phil was right. Maybe now, I wait to be found.
You have to let the flame lick your fingers sometimes
Even if you can't put your hand on the wick.

# Follow-Up Interview:
## On Sleeplessness, Possession

*Oh, you speak to me in riddles*
*And you speak to me in rhymes*
*My body aches to breathe your breath*
*Your words keep me alive*
  —Sarah McLachlan, "Possession"


This interview takes place
In my living room. I am surrounded
By art from my friends, paintings
Of space and Palisades Park and scarecrows,
How good it is to be alive, how rich.
Dr. Phil is sitting cross-legged
On the chair Grace usually sits on,
So I know there are socks and pens
And other paraphernalia of being a teenager
Underneath his large frame. "Should I
Lie down?" I ask, and he says, "If you wish."

I don't actually know what he's going
To ask this time. The other interviews,
There were cameramen and emails—
Heads up, it's time to talk about the fire,
About your broken, rubber-band body.
He takes a deep breath.
"Why are you so tired today?"

I open my mouth and he says, "Don't give me
some diagnosis. What happened in your sleep?"
My husband actually recorded it:
I slept with the arm I still can't feel
Straight up, or pulling my ear. I snored,
But only five times a minute. The spaces
Between my breaths were like chasms.
I could tell Andy was scared.

"No one wants to hear about dreams,"
I say, but he motions to get on with it.
"Fine. I was lost in the jungle,
And there was a snake. I'm good
With them—I handle them every
Time there's a chance. I wear
A string of rattlesnake vertebrae
Around my wrist. And this snake
Told me I looked so tired, to sleep,
He'd tell me a story. Set it up
Like the Odyssey: a hero writes
Love letters to the woman
Back home, who never does anything
But wait. The words sound
So familiar, but I can't place
Them—and then—I'm asleep—
I'm awake—he's around my neck—"
Dr. Phil cuts me off. "You can't sleep
When you're constantly being chased."

"That's the thing," I say. "I knew
The words, and I believed him
When he said it was a hero's arc.
But they were the lyrics to a song
That was written using excerpts
From a stalker's letter. It's a journeyman narrative,
But there's no hero." Dr. Phil nods.

"So who is the possessor and who
Is the possessed? You've always
Seen yourself as the tough guy."

It's just now that I'm realizing
I'm alone in my house with a man,
And though I trust Phil, this is a first.
I start to focus on anything I can
To keep the room from spinning:
The egg-covered breakfast dishes still
On the table. The computer.
An etching called "Sons of God"
Sent to me by a close friend.
"The song is called 'Possession,'"
I choke out. "Lately I feel possessed,
Like someone else has control
Of my right side, and I have to fight
To stay even half myself. And I'm
So damned tired."

              "But a snake,"
Phil says. "Didn't that seem dangerous?
Didn't those words trigger
Something in you?" He's right,
As always: they did, even though
I didn't place them until I woke up.
"I was too tired to care," I say.
Dr. Phil nods. "You have to start
Staying out of the woods—
I know you want to go to those places,
But it's not safe for you, not since the stroke."

I want to lash out. Scream. Throw
Something expensive, but what do I have?
Of course I already knew that. But
I wanted him to tell me that
Being willing to look at the snake
Meant I was going to get my old body
Back, even though, honestly,
The dream shook me. "It's been
Almost two years," I plead.
"How long until I can be normal again?"
Dr. Phil looks down. "Imagine
You are a doll, and you're stapled
Up the middle. Some things never change.
Maybe now you have staples
Up your belly, down your spine."
And they weren't literal—but as he said it,
I could feel the recoil of a staple gun
Against my skin, cold and precise,
And only painful on my left. On the right,
A slithering line of phantom
Anxiety where the pain should go,
All the way up to my neck.
Holding me together in the scariest way.

I AM NOT GIVING UP ON YOU

# Dr. Phil and Me Before the War

*after "Mont Blanc" by the Quiet Hollers*

"The bomb," Dr. Phil says. "We don't
Have much time." Of course it's delusion.
Where is my husband? My stepdaughter?
But he says, "You're learning to fly,
Bird brittle bones, filled with aerodynamic
Holes. You are learning how to split
Into pieces. But we don't have time now."

Of course there'd be a bunker
Under the soundstage, and the further
Down we get, the more I feel instability
At the core of the earth, thunder
In the soles of my shoes. I don't dare
Ask why he doesn't bring his family.
I don't dare mention that if this is really
*It,* a bunker won't save California
From sinking into the ocean, his tie bobbing
Up and down, my glasses with Prism
Lenses to focus my stroke-strained
Pupil floating away as we fade.

"So I'm in pieces," I say. "Why?"
He puts his big hand on my shoulder,
A feeling I've come to crave.
"You're learning how to tell yourself
The story of your own history," he says,
And with deep sadness, "You can only
Process one trauma at a time."

I try to ask him, "So which one is the bomb?"
But my vocal chords, they freeze,
And the last thing I see is a starburst purple,
Deep teal and pink swirled into the middle,
And for a moment, everything smells
Like sulfur.
But as the noise echoes in the distance, Phil's grip
Tightens, as if neither of us can go home
Until I know what's wrong with me.

# Dr. Phil and I Pretend to Be Punks

It didn't take long for my tattoos
To accumulate: the makeup
To extend out past my eyelid
Further, further. Gold. Glitter. Dirty
Hair, bitten nails. A jacket I sewed,
A picture of '70s Bowie on the back
Using a hand crippled by neuropathy

Halfway between not holding the needle
At all and piercing through to bone.
I always liked my music with teeth,
And once I realized this body was
A loaner, I decked it out like a teenager's
Car, bumper stickers and flashy dice
Even as I knew the transmission wore
And the engine block wasn't steady.

My shoulder is dislocated again,
Phil. It came out, fell
In front of a student after I'd jammed
It back in as hard as I could. We've done
The shoulder. You know. And you know
I wear a set of figure-8 rings—my iron
Knuckles—so my fingers don't dislocate
And break. But I'll be damned
If I don't wear silver boots or glittered
Shoes and pretend it's an aesthetic,
A do-it-yourself ragdoll, body dressed
Half in braces and prosthetics,
Half in neon rock shirts. And I want
That: the contrast distracts me
From the tint in my glasses,
The sag in my eye. But when I saw you

Dressed in those fake tattoos, black
Eyeliner raccooned and lined to your cheeks,
It made me wonder if we all had designs
Drawn somewhere inside our skin, hidden
Maybe from even our own view, waiting
To poke through, crooked X's,
To rise up and scar, leaving color—
Too much color—and strange beauty
Only to the beholder. And yeah,
Yours was a joke. Sometimes I wonder
If I'm joking, too: choosing random things
That make me happy, no rhyme, no reason
Not on my face or in my brain or—
But it doesn't really matter. I sew,

I play guitar. I got good at drawing more eyeliner
On one eye to make it look more open.
I put glitter on everything. And when
There's no glitter left, when I can't
Bend to tie those shoes with my busted shoulder
And my fingers, already crooked—
I wear the slip-ons, the ones with Johnny Ramone
On them. The ones that say
"HEY HO LET'S GO" on the back.
The ones that make me feel like I'm choosing
To look like this. Like it could be a joke,
And you and I could just go to wardrobe,
Wash all this away, forget the memories
Etched into our cores like permanent ink.

# I Try to Explain a Recurring Dream to Dr. Phil

This could be a poem of titles: "Hey, Andy,
Come Look at This," what I said, every time
It played out in my dreams—
        Even though I didn't know an Andy yet.

        Or—"How Could I Be
Infertile—I Saw the Baby So Clearly," which sounds
Maudlin, but I am befuddled. I have wondered
Where the baby with the blond curls was for years.

"This Cannot Be My Child"—that's the best one.
Because my brain does not believe it. I look at the child
Across from me and know, logically, there's no way
Even though I've done the math—
                Seen the pictures

            Of a bright-eyed child.
Why does a brain discuss so little with a heart? Why
When I have access to Dr. Phil am I just stalling,
Saying other titles to distract *you* from the truth?

The truth is, Dr. Phil, I know I cannot adopt someone
Who is—always—claimed. "Please tell my heart," I beg,
"Please tell it this is wrong. It's not some dream
I had—this is a real person, I had nothing—
             Almost nothing—

            To do with—"
Dr. Phil shakes his head. "I wouldn't bring this to air,"
He says. "This is a private session." I remind him:
*No one will read this. I'm a poet. They already know*

*I invent narratives, and maybe they aren't even good.*
He says, "Fine. What do you want?" And I said, "Teach
Me to stop loving so much." Dr. Phil shakes his head sadly.
"I'm sorry," he says. "There is ache in love,"
                                         And I know he's right.

                        I take a deep breath.
In the dream, the baby is blowing bubbles. Perfect
Curls. My husband's hair, it's curly. But you're bored,
And you should be. Dreams—scratch those.

What I do know? I remember that arguing down the street
Holding a piece of pizza at midnight, Andy shaking his head
While a curly-headed kid and I loudly argued behind him—
Talking about the economics of the French Revolution—
That was the best part of the best week
                          Of my life. One of them,

                        At least. And from our
Room, separated from his couch by a thin door, we heard
Them talking, and with a smile, Andy said, "Go see." When I did,
They were still arguing in their sleep about the war. Love aches,
   burns.

# Dr. Phil Rides Shotgun

I don't know how I managed to slam
My Honda Fit into the handicapped
Sign so damned hard without leaving
A visible scar, something that proves
I did it. Like these tinted lenses,
Like the ring splints that keep fingers
From dislocating and breaking as I turn the wheel—
Like the blue sign on my rearview mirror, taunting
Me. "Why didn't you tell me I was so close?"
I ask Phil, watching him drum out a Nada Surf
Song on the glovebox, his huge frame
Shoved into my tiny car.

"You aren't close," he said. "You made it."
I want to shake his shoulders,
To say both of us know that's not
What I meant, I meant don't let me
Hit the sign, don't let me look sick,
Even when I feel so defeated
I can't believe I'm going to get out
And teach. What do I have to say?
Phil smiles. "I'm proud of you," he says,

And for a minute, his voice reminds me
Of my dad's, soft and slightly southern,
And I know he's trying to convince me
That all of this is OK. Me? I want that,
But I'm still messing up words,
Oversleeping, up all night worried
That I'll never live in my body again;
That I've finally become the alien
I always said I'd be.

# Dr. Phil and I Go Back to 2001 (For a Minute)

*When you're angry you're at your weakest because you are coming from a place of feeling victimized. Anger is an attack and protect mode when you are actually feeling hurt, fear, or frustration.*
—Dr. Phil

I would have been—you know what, let's talk
Age through the world. We are immediately
In front of my CD stand, a beautiful triple-
Pronged thing, something you'd see in a store—

And the stereo. Oh, God. The speakers were small
But loud, and so loud with my Sony Walkman
Headphones plugged in I could still hear from bed.
They were fuzzy, pilling like a sweater from my touch

Trying to feel the bass. I loved the way I could feel
Heartbeat in music. And Dr. Phil is here, now.
He probably was then. I do him the favor of letting
Him explore my collection quietly, nodding approval

And gazing with questions. I won't ask him to remind
Me when he left Oprah and became my friend-in-the-dark,
The reason I had a DVR but no winter coat in Illinois.
"What's this one?" he asks, and I look absently

At the familiar jewel-case, a picture of a woman
And a baby, her face the flash reflection of a camera bulb.
"Remy Zero," I say, and smile, and now I am 2001
And however old I am now, and I tell him to put it in—

Six-CD changer, baby, two tape decks so you could copy
Mixtapes—and put it on track eight. "Over the Rails
& Hollywood High." I'd always loved it, and I rode it
The same as always, air-drumming, the doctor smiling

At my abandon. I always, after a good song, explain
It to the person, I'm with, why it lights me inside
Like a Chinese lantern, why I can't help but celebrate—
But track nine rolls over, and I'd forgotten it was "Smile."

It thunders. "No," I said. "Not this one." It's such an explosion
Into the room, he looks confused. "But I want to hear—"
Now I am in today again. We're ghosts in my old
Bedroom. "I said no." But reader—you know

It doesn't matter. Phil always gets to do what he wants.
Isn't this his story, anyway? If it's not, I can't hide
Behind his advice, pretend I don't need my imaginary
Friends still to get through the noise and chaos. So it plays.

"My heart just falls," it sings, "on every word you say—
And I will not fight, 'cause you will not listen." I don't want
To hear this one anymore. I don't know why. I touch
My shoulder and shake my head. "Have you heard enough?"

Dr. Phil says, "No." *You can cry if you want,* the song offers,
At the edge of Tate's range. "Smile?" Phil asks. I shake my head.
Is this where I learned it? The way to laugh off anything?
The way to hide my anxiety behind anger? The way

To punch a man to keep him out of a dressing room
Without thinking, even though my shoulder was already
In a sling? "It doesn't hurt," I say; I joke I'm the bouncer.
What a lie. Everything hurt. And though the song

Is about deciding when not to smile, I am broken
By the idea that I have to—always have to—choose.
A lot of times, I will say, "Do you want to hear something
Funny?" And if someone laughs with me, I know

They are, like me, sifting through something broken,
Something strange and foreign inside their heart,
Like maybe it was too big in the first place and someone
Else's sadness or glass shards got stuck there. Maybe it's this

Body, already a failure at 31. Maybe it's that I know
Every injury is a new baseline, a new forever. I will not
Smile. I will not smile. I—I smile. "I always loved this
Song, too," I tell Phil. "It's a little close to the razor."

So am I a victim? Because I'm furious that one by one,
Things stop working? That people need me to be strong,
Tell me I am, so that I have to become what I'm called?
Dr. Phil, your shoulder is back to normal: we dislocated

Them not many months apart. I see you wave with it.
I'm trying to learn to write with my left hand. Do you
Know the worst part? You're right. But I'll be damned
If I tell you, Phil, you're right: I'm not angry. I'm sad.

# Reading Over My Shoulder, Dr. Phil Asks Some Questions About Fire, Control

I've chosen a seat at a local coffee house: it's My Seat,
And I've sat here so long with real people that it's strange
To see Phil next to me today. I should be used to it by now.
"Hey," the text pops up on my phone, "How do you make

Flames turn blue? Green?" I go to answer from memory,
And the false-weight of pixels fall on my bad shoulder.
"How do you know that?" Dr. Phil asks. I smile. "There was
This house—everyone was always too drunk to see us sneak

To the second floor—if you pour—" I realize, I can't tell
Him the recipe. "We used to make a 'Tower of Flame,'"
I say. "Then, once the sparks would jump, crackle, color,
We'd leave the house, hordes of drunk college kids

Who didn't notice us in class and certainly didn't catch
Us in the frat. We never waited to see the sirens, flashing
Inevitably, the same color of our tower." He shakes his head.
"A dumb thing to tie police up with," he says. I agree—

"There was never a fire there once they arrived. Why bother?"
He shakes his head. I knew what he meant, but didn't care:
Why not have some fun? Why not be dumb and young? If I was
Too scared to drink or screw or even love, why not light

A tower that would embarrass a whole Fourth of July's worth
Of Roman candles? "It's not either/or," Dr. Phil says, but
I'm texting my student back. "I forget," I say. I don't, though.
What a relief, to remember a part of my past, to still have fire.

For fire to still be fun, not something that leaves College Katie's
Mementos in garage boxes, something that wakes me smelling
Smoke, ghost smoke, nothing real: but the tower. That was real.
It was a controlled burn. And if it wasn't, I was too dumb to know.

# Dr. Phil and I Watch My Husband Play Guitar in a Packed Bar

*Be careful what you wish for, friend*
*'Cos I've been to hell and back again*
*And I feel all right, I feel all right*
                              —Steve Earle


Andy worried about me making
the trip; I hadn't left the house much
since stroke rehab, and someone still
needed to hold my right side so I didn't slip left—

I think: *My body that is made, at least half,*
*Of Monday mornings, half of well-slept*
*Saturday afternoons, moving foot*
*After foot as if it were natural. So strange.*

But by this time, I need to move, still
surrounded by dying hospital flowers
and friends who clearly worried
I was dying. I was out of the eyepatch.
I wasn't on the walker. And Dr. Phil
reminded me, "Your husband
is right. You have to push boundaries
to know where they are."

That didn't make it easier for Andy
to tip the bartender to monitor
my pupil size, to know if I was too tired.
Buoyed with Mexican soft drinks in glass
bottles, Dr. Phil and I sat through warm-up,
both enjoying the Steve Earle cover.

But now it is late in the set, and I'm wobbling
on the smooth barstool, digging in my
*Aladdin Sane* bag, praying I brought
something to make me less dizzy. I swear
I could feel Phil try to comfort my right
side, the confused sensation of burning
and freezing, wondering why, at 31, I had
to say the word "stroke," so often.

*It's like the record didn't scratch, like
Andy never flung that Telecaster
closer and closer to the amp,
the feedback, the high-pitched sound
tearing me down the middle,* I scream,
and Phil nods back. "It's like always:
you look normal, so people don't understand
why you are the way you are, what's wrong
with you."

      "Sometimes I want to grab every person
I see and scream, 'You have no idea what I've
been through.'" Phil popped open another glass-
bottled Coke. I prayed he wouldn't say something
stupid like *We're all fighting our own battles*
or *What doesn't kill you makes you stronger.*
We look at each other, and I know he can tell
that I'd punch him as hard as I could with my good
side. "I feel all right," he sings along with Andy's
high harmony. I take the melody.
*I feel all right.*

# The Poem Where I Tell Dr. Phil He's Not Real

Of course he's real *some*where, but tonight
I don't want to think about my problems,
My failures. So I say the thing that will hurt
Him—the truest thing. He recoils like a person
Who has been told the worst news about themselves
But he knew all along, and he deflates
Like a plastic bag that the wind finally stops
Carrying. I feel bad for a moment, but he starts
Asking why I need to lash out when he only
Wants to help me, and then I remember why
I had to say it. As long as he was with me,
I had to live in my head—and I wanted
So bad to exist in the physical world again.
On the couch, I have four knitting
Projects spilled in colorful balls, waiting
For me to finish: I can't focus on one of them
Long enough to complete it before bright
Yarn distracts me to a new one. I want to drown
In the rich jewel tones, in the deep mustard yellows.
He asks if he can touch one, and I reluctantly
Agree, because he's fading away, becoming more
Of a ghost every second. He closes his eyes
And his fingers sink through one of the thicker
Scarves and suddenly, my heart feels like it will explode
With sorrow. He smiles, gently, and says, "You can't
See what you're not ready to see," and I want to scream,
*Come back please come back.* But that's the catch
With illusion: I was only hurting myself. He knew
He wasn't there all along, but I'd fallen for it:
Here, now, what should have hurt him
Left me empty.
          I yell, "I'm sorry," I yell,
"I can give another interview, I promise.

I'll tell you everything. The fire, the stroke—
Whatever you want to hear." I try to conjure
The soundstage, which seemed so easy before:
But my body, ripped into one side pain, one
Numb—I try to turn it into a thousand bluebird
Feathers and launch my weak bones transcontinental,

To the soundstage, but no matter how hard
I close my eyes, everything is black: no heat
From studio lights, no crush of sound from faceless
Audience, and no Texan greeting, no handshake.

# About the Author

Katie Darby Mullins teaches creative writing at the University of Evansville. In addition to being nominated for both the Pushcart Prize and Best of the Net multiple times, she's been published or has work forthcoming in journals like *Barrelhouse, The Rumpus, Iron Horse, Harpur Palate, Prime Number,* and the music magazines *The Aquarian* and *Paste,* as well as quoted in James Campion's recent book about "Hey Jude," *Take a Sad Song.* She helped found and is the executive writer for Underwater Sunshine Fest, a music festival in NYC, and her first book, *Neuro, Typical: Chemical Reactions & Trauma Bonds* came out on Summer Camp Press in late 2020. She also has column at *HAD* called "Things That Look More Like Me Than My Face."

www.ingramcontent.com/pod-product-compliance
Lightning Source LLC
Chambersburg PA
CBHW030908170426
43193CB00009BA/780